INVENTORS
AND INVENTIONS

MICHAEL JEFFRIES AND GARY A. LEWIS

SMITHMARK

About the authors

Michael Jeffries is a former journalist who now works as a free-lance writer and editor. For more than 20 years, he has written about science, technology, and medicine. Mr. Jeffries was medical and science correspondent of London's *Evening Standard* newspaper and editor of *Science & Business*, a magazine devoted to innovations and inventions for commercial use. Before this, he was editor of *Family Business* and is the author of *Know Your Body*.

Gary A. Lewis is a children's author who has written more than 50 books and television scripts. Mr. Lewis received a graduate degree in English literature from Columbia University. He lives with his wife and two children in New York City.

Editor:
Philip de Ste. Croix

Designer:
Stonecastle Graphics Ltd

Picture research:
Leora Kahn

Coordinating editors:
Andrew Preston
Kristen Schilo

Production:
Ruth Arthur
Sally Connolly
Neil Randles

Production editor:
Didi Charney

Production director:
Gerald Hughes

Typesetter:
Pagesetters Incorporated

Color and monochrome reproduction:
Advance Laser Graphic Arts, Hong Kong

Text copyright © 1992 SMITHMARK
Publishers Inc./Michael Jeffries

This edition published in 1996 by SMITHMARK Publishers, a division of U.S. Media Holdings, Inc., 16 East 32nd Street, New York NY 10016

SMITHMARK books are available for bulk purchase for sales promotion and premium use. For details write or call the manager of special sales, SMITHMARK Publishers, Inc. 16 East 32nd Street, New York, NY 10016; (212) 532-6600

Produced by CLB Publishing
Godalming Business Centre
Woolsack Way, Godalming, Surrey, UK

Printed in China

10 9 8 7 6 5 4 3 2

Library of Congress Cataloging-in-Publication Data

Jeffries, Michael.
    Facts America. Inventors and inventions / Michael Jeffries & Gary
A. Lewis.
        p. cm.
    Includes bibliographical references and index.
    Summary: Discusses the accomplishments of men and women who have given us important inventions in such areas as industry and commerce, weapons and warfare, and communication.
    ISBN 0-8317-5366-8 (hardcover)
    1. Inventions—United States—Juvenile literature. 2. Inventors—United States—Juvenile literature. [1. Inventors. 2. Inventions.]
I. Lewis, Gary A., 1950–   II. Title. III. Title:
Inventors and inventions.
T21.J44 1992
609.73—dc20   92-9402

The famous inventor Thomas A. Edison, pictured in October 1911 in West Orange, New Jersey. He is seen with a phonograph, the forerunner of the record player, which he invented when he was only 30 years old.

Contents

Yale graduate Eli Whitney (1765–1825) was working as a tutor at a plantation when his employer encouraged him to try to find a fast way to separate cotton fibers from their seeds. In 1793, Whitney designed the cotton gin (short for engine). His invention consisted of a cylinder with teeth that revolved against a grate that contained the cotton. The teeth caught the cotton fibers and pulled them from the seeds.

The cotton gin sped up the process of separating cotton from its seeds so much that the Cotton Belt, which formerly consisted only of South Carolina and Georgia, grew to encompass the area of South Virginia to east Texas.

Whitney patented the cotton gin in 1794. But because the concept was so simple, his patents were violated by other manufacturers. Although he received royalties and a $50,000 payment from the state of South Carolina for his invention, virtually all the money was spent on legal fees protecting it.

Whitney later made another fortune, selling 10,000 mass-produced guns to the U.S. government. Mass-produced guns have interchangeable parts, which means they can be manufactured quickly. Whitney won the order when he threw down a pile of mixed components in front of a government official and then assembled a weapon from the heap.

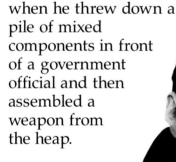

▲ *A poster from the 1860s of Elias Howe and his sewing machine, which revolutionized fashion—yet found few backers when first invented.*

◀ *Eli Whitney gave up plans to become a lawyer to invent the cotton gin and "mix and match" weapon parts. On the way, he made and lost a fortune.*

▼ *Howe exhibited his first lock-stitch sewing machine in 1845. This is a version of that first sewing machine.*

Elias Howe: Sewing machine

Handmade clothing is slow and expensive to make. Without the sewing machine, few of us would be able to afford the clothes we wear. A German hosiery worker named Balthazar Krems first invented a chain-stitch sewing machine in 1810. It used a needle with an eye near its point to deliver a loop of thread through fabric. Walter Hunt, the American inventor of the safety pin, then designed the first lock-stitch sewing machine in 1833. Turning its handle operated a needle and eye that inserted loops of thread through the material. The stitch was "locked" in place by a shuttle underneath, which fed a second thread through the loop of the first to form an interlocking stitch. But although Hunt sold the device to a manufacturer, it was never developed.

In 1838, Elias Howe (1819–67) was apprenticed to a Boston instrument- and watchmaker who encouraged him to devise a sewing machine. Unaware of Hunt's machine, Howe built a similar device that sewed seven times faster than by hand. But Howe could not find financial backing for his machine, which was patented in the United States in 1846. So he went to England and sold his second sewing machine to William Thomas.

Their partnership was not a success. Penniless, Howe returned to the United States in 1847, only to find that others had pirated his design and were manufacturing and selling his machines. Howe launched court actions against competitors, including engineer Isaac Merrit Singer. Howe won a patent infringement action in 1854, and for the 13 years until his death, he was paid royalties by Singer. Howe died a wealthy man.

Singer, who in 1860 went into partnership to start the Singer and Clark Machine Company, became the world's largest manufacturer of sewing machines.

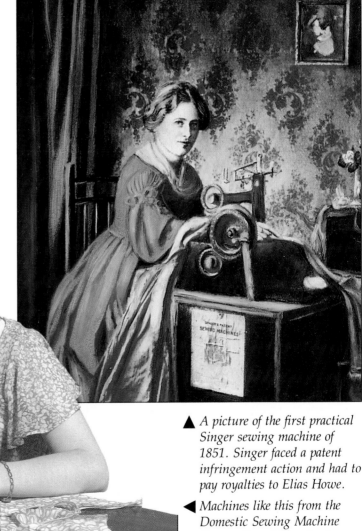

▲ A picture of the first practical Singer sewing machine of 1851. Singer faced a patent infringement action and had to pay royalties to Elias Howe.

◄ Machines like this from the Domestic Sewing Machine Corporation of Cleveland enabled women to make dresses at home quickly and cheaply.

Thomas Edison: Inventor extraordinary

Thomas Edison ▶ in his chemistry laboratory in West Orange, N.J. Among the 1,000-plus inventions of this home-educated genius were the record player, the light bulb, and motion pictures.

Thomas Alva Edison (1847–1931) was a giant among inventors. He patented over 1,000 inventions, including the record player, "moving pictures," and the first practical electric light. Largely home taught, Edison only went to school for three months in 1854. But he displayed his genius early. At 17, he invented the quadruplex telegraph system. This allowed four dot-dash messages to be sent down a wire simultaneously, speeding up telegraph service enormously.

Edison's first commercially successful invention was for Wall Street. He was hired to fix a faulty stock market ticker-tape machine transmitting gold prices at the Gold Indicator Company. He then built his own improved version and sold it to Western Union for $40,000. Edison used the money to hire a technical team and establish workshops in Newark, New Jersey. He moved to Menlo Park in 1876. A year later, he invented the record player, then called the phonograph, or gramophone. Recordings were made on revolving horizontal metal cylinders and played back by a needle running through the grooves.

▲ The exhausted inventor was photographed after working nonstop five days and nights to finish his favorite invention: the phonograph.

Thomas Edison's basic ▶ incandescent electric lamp, patented in 1880. Two years later, New York became the first city to be lit by electricity.

▲ A modern electric light bulb. A filament of tungsten in argon gas replaces Edison's original carbon filament in a glass vacuum.

◀ Edison experiments with his first motion picture machine in 1905. He also introduced 35mm cine film with perforations on both edges.

There was no stopping Edison's genius, and he often worked up to 20 hours a day. In 1879, he discovered that if electric current is passed through a thin thread of carbon in a glass vacuum, it becomes white hot, giving off a brilliant light. Then, for use with this electric light, he developed a complete electrical distribution system. In 1878, he formed the Edison Electric Light Company. In 1882, he built the Pearl Street plant, and New York became the first city lit by electricity.

Edison later invented coin-operated Kinetoscopes showing "moving pictures." He also worked on synchronizing motion pictures and sound; talking pictures were based on this work. And he developed the perforated edges of celluloid movie film, which control its projection speed more effectively.

Edwin Drake: Oil-drilling rig

The world's first recorded search for oil was with a rig erected by G. C. Hunaus near Hanover, Germany, in 1857. But Edwin Drake (1819–1880) of Greenville, New York, a one-time railroad construction worker, launched the modern petroleum industry with his pioneering drilling operations at Titusville, Pennsylvania.

Working for industrialist George Henry Bissell, Drake persuaded the Pennsylvania Rock Oil Company, which gathered surface seepage oil for medicinal uses, to lease him part of their land at Titusville for drilling. Adapting methods of drilling for salt, he bored a hole by hammering a metal shaft with a heavy tool powered by a steam engine. This broke up, rather than cut, the rock. Despite some ridicule, in 1859, Drake struck oil at a depth of 69 feet, creating the first producing oil well in the United States. Oil found a ready market, particularly as a cheaper form of lamp and heating oil; the age of the gasoline-driven automobile was still 25 years off.

Drake lost his money in further oil speculation. Despite the oil boom in Pennsylvania, he lived in poverty after failing to patent his drilling system. But he was finally awarded a state pension.

▲ A modern oil rig uses drilling bits fixed to lengths of pipe slung from a derrick. New, unmanned sea platforms can pump 70,000 barrels of oil daily.

▲ Edwin Drake, the man who started the oil rush. Although his strike was small, it marked the beginning of the modern petroleum industry.

◀ This drawing, based on a photograph, shows Edwin Drake in front of the first oil well. Doubters dubbed it Drake's Folly.

Lucien Smith: Barbed wire

Films that depict how the West was won do not give enough credit to one of the major players: barbed wire. After the Civil War ended in 1865, farmers and cattlemen began driving west to establish farms and ranches in the rich agricultural prairie lands. With few natural fencing materials to keep their cattle safely away from crops, they turned to the brainchild of one Lucien Smith. In 1867, he had patented the simple idea that was quickly recognized as solving the problem: an artificial "thorn hedge" consisting of wire with short metal spikes twisted on by hand at regular intervals.

Sales were so great that barbed wire could not be made fast enough. In the 1870s, Joseph Farwell Glidden (1813–1906), a 60-year-old farmer, invented a machine that put the barbs on to barbed wire. Thus, Smith and Glidden advanced the settlement of the American continent.

Barbed wire is quite effective at keeping *humans* in or out, too. It was used in large coils to fence off trenches and military bases during both world wars, and continues to be used as a security measure throughout the world.

▲ *Stretching barbed wire taut before fixing it to a fence post. Barbed wire is extremely effective at keeping animals and humans in or out.*

▼ *Cattle grazed just about anywhere before the advent of barbed wire. When invented, it could not be made fast enough.*

▼ *The remains of Drake's oil well in Titusville, Pennsylvania. A tablet on a nearby stone marks the spot where he sank his exploratory shaft in 1859.*

▼ *Not everyone was sold on barbed wire. The English huntsman's opposition is depicted in this humorous* Punch *magazine cartoon: "The Modern Fox Hunter Equipped Against the Modern Fence."*

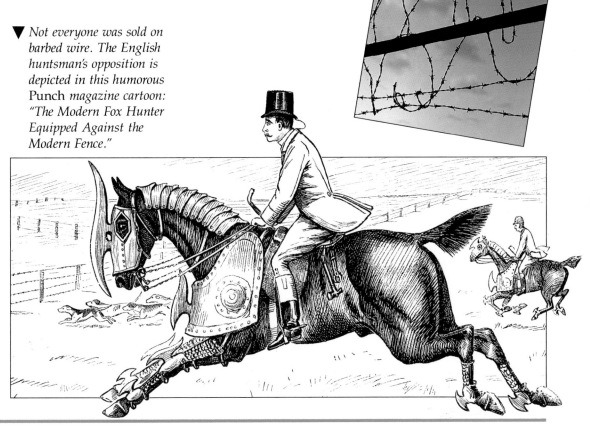

Christopher Sholes: Typewriter

The first patent for a typewriter was taken out by one Henry Mill in England in 1714. Another early "writing machine" was built in 1808 by an Italian, Pellegrino Turri of Castelnuovo, so that a blind countess friend could write letters. In fact, early models of the typewriter were primarily for the blind. But in 1866, Christopher Latham Sholes (1819–90), the editor of a Milwaukee newspaper, teamed up with Carlos Glidden and Samuel W. Soulé to create the first practical commercial typewriter. A gun and sewing machine company, Remington Small Arms, bought the manufacturing rights and marketed Sholes's typewriter in 1874. The typewriter not only revolutionized office work but created a social revolution as well. Typing provided paid employment for many women who went out to work for the first time.

Sholes got the idea for his typewriter by watching someone play the piano. Today's typewriters still work on the same basic principles used in his early machine. Sholes first arranged his typewriter keys in alphabetical order but soon found that the most frequently used letters got in one another's way and jammed. His QWERTY system—named from the order of the first six letters—solved the problem by spreading them widely on the keyboard. It is still used today.

In 1883, Mark Twain became the first writer to type an entire book on the typewriter.

▲ *Sholes's typewriter. Hitting a key caused a letter character to strike the paper through an inked ribbon. This printed the character on the paper, which then advanced a space.*

◀ *Nimble fingers are able to type at high speeds because the QWERTY keyboard spreads the workload evenly.*

▲ *A stenographer in 1902 taking dictation before typing her letters. Mark Twain's* Life on the Mississippi *was typed on a Remington.*

James Ritty: Cash register

James Ritty (1836–1918), who ran a popular bar in Dayton, Ohio, was making himself ill worrying about stealing by his bartenders. During a cruise to Europe for his health, he saw a device aboard the ship that counted the number of revolutions of the ship's propeller. Using a similar idea, he and his mechanic brother, John, designed the first cash register in 1879.

Ritty's cash register consisted of a metal device like a clockface with two rows of typewriterlike keys below it. The clockface had two hands. When the cost of each drink was "rung up" on the keys, the small hand registered the dollars on an inner ring on the clockface, while the large hand recorded cents on an outer ring. Inside the machine were two disks that added up the total sale.

Ritty patented his cash register and sold the rights to a group that formed the National Cash Register Company in 1884. They made further improvements, such as adding receipts.

▼ *Ritty's invention caught on in Europe. Here are cash registers being assembled in the German Krupp factory to meet a growing demand.*

▲ *This is not a clock. It's the first dial cash register of James Ritty made by the National Cash Register Company. When a sale was made, the outer ring recorded cents and the inner registered dollars.*

◄ *An old-style cash register of 1890. Many such machines were in use until after World War II. Ringing up the total flagged the amount in a window, opened the cash drawer, and recorded the sale.*

▲ *Today, many stores use cash registers that are computerized. An LED display shows the price and total cost of items bought.*

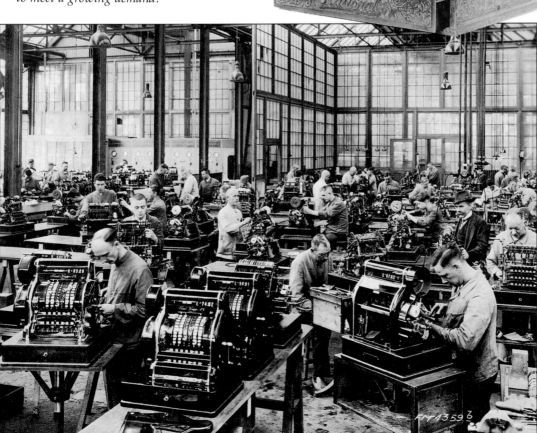

Chester Carlson: Photocopier

Working in the patent department of the Bell Research Laboratories in New York, Chester Floyd Carlson (1906–68) knew how difficult it was to copy documents. They usually had to be manually retyped or photographed, which could take days. In 1935, he began to develop an idea for a copying machine. He printed his first copy on October 22, 1938, and patented his ideas in 1940.

Carlson's machine was based on the fact that positive and negative electric charges attract each another. A drum covered with a thin layer of an element called selenium was given an electric charge. Selenium holds an electric charge in the dark but loses this charge where light falls on it. The original document was then reflected by a mirror onto the drum. Where the light parts of the document were reflected onto the drum, the selenium lost its positive charge. Where the dark parts were reflected, the charge remained.

Next, the drum was dusted with a dark powder carrying a negative charge. The powder stuck only to the dark, positively charged areas. Then the copying paper made contact with the drum. Because the paper was positively charged, it attracted the powder—creating an image on the paper. Heat melted the powder, fusing the image to the paper and making a clear copy of the original document.

Twenty companies refused to market Carlson's invention over the next six years. Finally, in 1947, the small Haloid Company of Rochester, New York, bought the rights to the dry copying process. It was called xerography, from the Greek words meaning "dry writing." Haloid grew to become the giant Xerox Corporation.

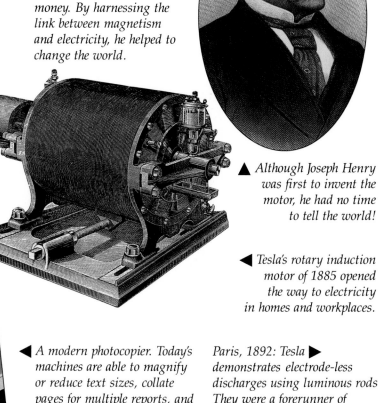

▲ Nikola Tesla arrived in the United States with little money. By harnessing the link between magnetism and electricity, he helped to change the world.

▲ Although Joseph Henry was first to invent the motor, he had no time to tell the world!

◀ Tesla's rotary induction motor of 1885 opened the way to electricity in homes and workplaces.

◀ A modern photocopier. Today's machines are able to magnify or reduce text sizes, collate pages for multiple reports, and copy in color.

Paris, 1892: Tesla ▶ demonstrates electrode-less discharges using luminous rods. They were a forerunner of today's fluorescent lighting.

Nikola Tesla: Electric motor

Without electric motors, we wouldn't have washing machines, refrigerators, video, electric drills, and many other useful household items. Cars would not start easily, elevators would never get off the ground floor, and industry would grind to a halt. Such is the importance of electric motors, which transform electrical energy into mechanical energy—the energy that can actually move things.

In 1820, Hans Christian Øersted (1777–1851), a Danish scientist, discovered the fact upon which all electric motors are based: the link between electric current and magnetism. He found that an electric current flowing through a wire makes the wire a magnet for as long as the current flows through it.

Nikola Tesla (1856–1943) was a Croatian-born engineering genius. He reputedly arrived in America from Europe with only a few cents and a knowledge of 12 languages. In 1881, Tesla conceived of using an alternating current (ac) to produce an electric motor. Alternating current is current that continually reverses its direction of flow. In contrast, direct current flows in one direction only.

The simplest electric motor consists of a coil of wire attached to a shaft. At opposite ends of the coil are two magnets that remain fixed. One magnet has its south pole facing the coil. The other has its north pole facing the coil. When an electric current is passed through the coil, the coil becomes magnetized. Because like poles, e.g.,

north and north, repel—and unlike poles, e.g., north and south, attract—the magnetized coil swings around until its south pole lines up with the magnet whose north pole faces it, and vice versa.

At this point, the direction of the electric current being passed through the coil is reversed. This reverses the magnetic poles of the coil. North becomes south, and south becomes north. The coil therefore spins around so that its "new" north and south poles line up with the magnets of opposite polarity. Reversing the current several times per second makes the coil spin rapidly.

Tesla's motor introduced a special refinement. In his motor, the coils were fixed and the permanent magnet rotated. What's more, Tesla used more than two coils. These coils were positioned in a circle around the rotating permanent magnet much like the numbers on a clock are fixed around its rotating hands. The idea was to produce a rotating magnetic field. This would cause each pole of the rotating permanent magnet to "chase" a moving pole of opposite type.

Tesla did this by passing electricity flowing in the correct direction to each fixed coil in turn, which created the rotating magnetic field. This made the motion of his motor smoother than that of a motor with one coil.

At the time of his invention, Tesla was working for Thomas Edison as a research assistant. But Edison favored a direct current (dc) system for generators and motors. Tesla therefore sold his alternating current system to the American industrialist George Westinghouse. The superiority of Tesla's system was confirmed when it was chosen to power the Niagara Falls hydroelectric station.

Actually, Tesla was not the only one with an idea for an electric motor. The distinguished American inventor Joseph Henry (1797–1878) is said to have produced the first practical design for an electric motor in about 1830. Due to teaching pressures, however, he did not publish his findings for five years. Henry also invented the telegraph in 1831.

Ottmar Mergenthaler: Linotype

The words you are now reading owe their existence in part to Ottmar Mergenthaler (1854–99), a German working in America. In 1886, he invented the Linotype machine, which ended the need to assemble individual letters and spaces by hand. The operator sat down at a typewriterlike keyboard. As the keys were tapped, molds for each letter and space were brought together to automatically cast a complete line of type in metal. The Linotype provided high-speed typesetting for newspaper and book publishers. First to use it was the New York *Tribune*.

Hot on Mergenthaler's heels with a similar machine, called a Monotype, was Tolbert Lanston (1844–1913), an American civil servant. His device, invented in 1887, first translated words onto a punched tape. The tape was then fed into the machine, which cast the type in metal. Although too slow for many newspapers, Monotype produced higher-quality type, and the book industry adopted it. This hot-metal typesetting has now been replaced by computerized typesetting.

◄ *Ottmar Mergenthaler demonstrates his machine to set type quickly to Whitelaw Reid at the New York* Tribune. *The* Tribune *was the first newspaper to use it.*

▼ *Technology has moved on. Type is now set and printing machines run by computer. This web offset litho machine prints at very high speeds.*

▼ *Bakelite, named after its inventor Leo Baekeland, found its way into many products, from radio cabinets and ornaments to "sturdy pools and playthings."*

▲ *Ottmar Mergenthaler, the "father of mechanical typesetting." Today, hot-metal type is seldom used.*

◄ *This sheet-fed press from the early part of the century printed newspapers from texts set mechanically on Linotype and Monotype machines.*

Leo Baekeland: Plastic

Wallace Carothers: Nylon

When Leo Hendrik Baekeland (1863–1944), a Belgian-American, produced Bakelite in 1909, it was nothing like the synthetic shellac substance he had been trying to make. What could this hard, amber-colored resin he had created be used for?

He did not realize it until later, but Baekeland had stumbled on the world's first heat-proof plastic. The resin he produced could be cast, machined, and was durable. Bakelite was widely used because of its electrical insulation properties, as well as for making articles such as ashtrays and radio cabinets. Baekeland's company, the General Bakelite Corporation, eventually merged with others to become a subsidiary of Union Carbide. In 1899, he was paid $1 million by Kodak for another invention, a photographic paper called Velox.

◀ *Leo Baekeland, the man who accidentally invented heat-proof plastic. Born in Belgium, he settled in the United States after a honeymoon tour.*

Nylon stockings made ▶ *in America were a symbol of luxury for European women during World War II. Parachutes made from the tough thread helped the war effort.*

Nylon is similar to protein in its chemical structure. It is used in the manufacture of textiles, where it has properties as good as or better than silk, cotton, and wool. Nylon may be used for simulated furs and silks, clothes, carpets, parachutes, medical sutures, and many other products. Wallace Hume Carothers (1896–1937), born in Burlington, Iowa, led the research team at E. I. Du Pont de Nemours and Co. that invented nylon in 1935. His invention laid the foundations for the man-made fiber industry, which produces nylon stockings and other clothes for women. Sadly, despite his success, Carothers suffered a depressive illness and committed suicide two years after nylon was patented.

Around the Home Hamilton Smith: Washing machine

Until the invention of the washing machine, clothes had been washed in tubs of one sort or another for thousands of years. Often, a stick known as a wash dolly was used to agitate the clothes and help clean them.

In 1858, Hamilton Smith, a manufacturer from Pittsburgh, Pennsylvania, produced a laborsaving washing machine. In one model, the operator turned a handle to revolve the dolly, which was inside a vertical wooden drum containing the clothes and water. Later, Smith added a refinement that allowed the user to agitate the clothes backward and forward as well.

With increasing industrialization, the early 20th century was a golden time for inventors in America. This was particularly true for those producing laborsaving devices for the home. So when Alva Fisher of Chicago designed the first electric washing machine, there was considerable interest. Basically, it was a motorized version of the hand-cranked machine, except the clothes drum was positioned horizontally.

In 1924, the Savage Arms Corporation produced an advanced machine that combined washing and spin drying. First you washed the clothes in the tub, which rotated slowly at 45 degrees. Then you lifted the drum and placed it vertically onto another, faster system that spun the wash dry.

Electric water heaters and pumps were introduced in the 1940s, and tumble dryers incorporating hot-air blowers came a decade later. The latest machines merely have to be loaded with laundry. Push a few buttons, and your wash is done!

▲ *Much of the drudgery of laundering for women in the 1870s ended with the manufacture of rudimentary washing machines, like the one shown here.*

◄ *A range of washing machines from bygone days. Rocking Old Faithful's lever moved twin paddles inside the machine, which safely washed even "the daintiest" garments.*

For those without washing ▶ machines, a new "industry" of Laundromats was born.

An ad for soap being ▶ filmed in yesterday's dream kitchen. A key prop is one of the newest washing machines of the day, complete with wringer.

Machines that washed the ▶ clothes did only half the job. Soon there was a demand for electric dryers, so that the clothes came out ready to iron. Here, a woman takes towels from her Westinghouse dryer. Modern machines are controlled by computer chips.

Linus Yale: Cylinder lock

Few people go through a day without turning a key in a lock. Although locks date back to about 2500 B.C., the age of mass production required a lock whose parts could be duplicated by the thousands. But each lock had to require its own key!

Linus Yale, Jr. (1821–68), a Philadelphia locksmith, solved the problem. His pin tumbler lock design, patented in 1851, is still widely used today. The Yale lock consists of about five pins, or tumblers, held down by springs. When the key is inserted, each pin is lifted a different amount according to the serrated pattern of the key. If the key matches the lock, the movements of the pins as the key is turned brings them all into alignment. This allows the cylinder to turn and withdraw the bolt.

Yale's lock cannot be picked easily and is often used for car ignition locks.

The machine-made Clinton safety pin in this advertisement was patented by the Oakville Company in ▶ 1881.

◀ *Typical Yale locks. They can ▼ be mass produced, are difficult to pick, and are often used for car ignition locks.*

Walter Hunt: Safety pin

New York draftsman Walter Hunt (1796–1859) deserves our admiration—and our sympathy. The story goes that in 1849, he owed a colleague $15 but was completely broke when asked to repay the loan. He saw no way of getting the money together . . . until he began doodling on his drawing board. Crude fastening pins had been around for about 1,500 years, but not like the one that Hunt sketched. His had a simple coil spring at one end to hold the point firmly in the safety sleeve covering the other.

Hunt found a piece of wire and quickly shaped it into a working model. The same day, Hunt sold the patent rights for $100 and repaid his friend, keeping $85 for himself. The safety pin went on to make a fortune for its patent holders. It is still as useful today as it was then.

CLINTON SAFETY PINS

. . . RUSTPROOF

. . . ADDED STRENGTH

. . . GUARDED COILS

Do you perchance recognize the two left-hand illustrations? They appeared in a Scovill advertisement in *Time* magazine on May 31. If you didn't read it at that time . . . you may find it worth your while to turn back to that issue. The early history of the safety pin is interestingly told.

[... quo]te in part: "Safety pins of the common [... ope]n variety, as distinct from ornamental [...] a comparatively modern invention. Their [... is] practically the history of the Oakville [... y] . . . It was not until 1881 that an auto[...]ly made, practical safety pin was patented,

and this was the Clinton pin. This was the first pin that could be fastened and unfastened on either side. Later the Clinton was still further improved by adding a metal guard over the coil end of the pin—which prevents fabrics from catching. These two changes are probably the only two major improvements that have ever been made in the common safety pin."

The Clinton 10c and Eldorado 5c notion lines are complete. They give you a complete stock on a single order,—thus saving you separate shipping charges and duplication of orders. Write today for full information.

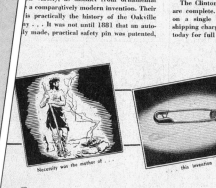
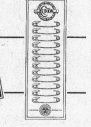

Necessity was the mother of . . .   . . . this invention

OAKVILLE COMPANY

SAFETY PINS, PINS, SNAP FASTENERS, HOOKS & EYES, THIMBLES, SHOE LACES, NEEDLES

DIVISION SCOVILL MFG. CO.   NEW YORK—CHICAGO
OAKVILLE, CONNECTICUT   SAN FRANCISCO

"INSIST ON OAKVILLE ● YOUR CUSTOMERS DO!"

Lewis Waterman: Fountain pen

▼ *Lewis Waterman's fountain pen factory in New York around the turn of the century. Today, the ballpoint has mostly replaced the fountain pen.*

(Right) *Stages in the making* ▶ *of a pen nib.* (Far right) *A pen's components, showing the rubber reservoir that holds the ink and the polished pen casing*

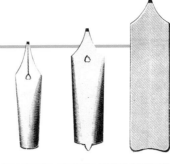

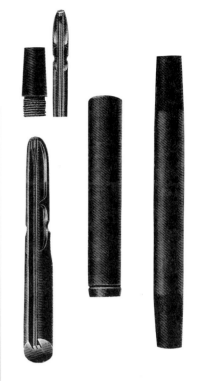

▼ *A modern Waterman fountain pen. High-speed stenographers often use these; they produce extremely clear characters.*

Pens with their own supplies of ink were a big improvement on simple quills. They date back at least 300 years. Samuel Pepys, the English diarist, recorded having had a fountain pen in 1663. There are also records of a fountain pen's being manufactured in 1809. Ink was poured into a silver tube attached to a quill nib. Because there was no hole in the tube to prevent air locks, the writer had to squeeze the tube periodically to maintain a supply of ink. Often, he squeezed too hard—and "blotted his copybook."

An American insurance salesman, Lewis Edson Waterman (1837–1901), spotted the problem and designed the first successful fountain pen, which allowed air into the barrel as the ink flowed out. It was filled by an eyedropper after unscrewing the barrel. Improvements in filling the pen were made in later designs. A long bar inside the barrel squeezed the air from a rubber tube when a small lever was pulled. When the nib was held in ink and the lever released, the ink was forced up into the tube by the action of atmospheric pressure.

George Eastman: Kodak camera

Photography was invented in the first half of the 19th century. But it was complicated and expensive. George Eastman (1854–1932), a photographic dry-plate manufacturer in Rochester, New York, turned everyone into photographers when he launched his popular Kodak camera in 1888. The Kodak (a made-up name) was the first to use rolls of film on which a number of pictures could be exposed. Before, cameras had used one cumbersome glass plate for each picture. Plus, the Kodak sold for only $25!

The camera was basically a lightproof box with a lens at the front and film at the back. When the user clicked the shutter, the lens opened and a burst of light from the subject struck the film, which was coated with light-reacting chemicals. This created an image.

Four years before launching his camera, Eastman had invented a flexible roll-film system. His patent in 1884 was for a paper-backed film coated with a light-sensitive gel emulsion. This was replaced five years later with coated celluloid film, which was cheaper to process and made photography even more popular. But Eastman did not want to baffle his customers with science. His shrewd sales pitch: "You press the button— we do the rest."

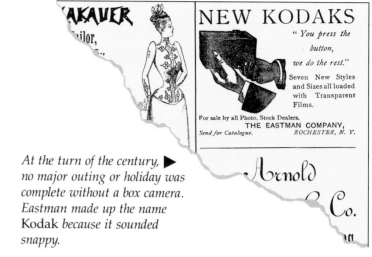

At the turn of the century, ▶ no major outing or holiday was complete without a box camera. Eastman made up the name Kodak *because it sounded snappy.*

These famous ▶ inventors are George Eastman, also an industrialist, and Thomas Edison, who invented a number of film techniques.

◀ Box cameras were joined by more compact cameras with folding bellows, as shown in this advertisement, circa 1910, entitled "The Kodak Girl."

Edwin Land: Polaroid camera

▲ *Edwin Land with his Polaroid camera. He was the first person to build a camera that developed and printed the picture instantly.*

Click! *And the Polaroid* ▲ *Spectra QPS processes and prints the picture before your eyes. Land also invented Polaroid sunglasses.*

Edwin Herbert Land (1909–91), a physicist and inventor, was a Harvard dropout. But this did not stop him from going on to invent the instant camera and Polaroid sunglasses.

Cameras use light and chemicals to produce a photograph. In 1947, Land found a way of doing away with the secondary stage of developing and printing the picture by incorporating the whole process within the film. Polaroid cameras use special film that contains its own developing and fixing chemicals. When the film is pulled from the camera or ejected by a tiny built-in motor, these chemicals start reacting to produce the finished picture within a minute.

Prior to this, in the 1930s, Land capitalized on the fact that rays of a shaft of light vibrate at random angles to the beam. Physicists have long known that if certain transparent crystals are placed in front of a light beam, only those rays vibrating in the same plane as the crystals will

pass through. This is called polarization. Land's Polaroid sunglasses are coated with a synthetic sheet of plastic that polarizes light—and cuts out glare. A similar coating is also used for car windshields, headlight lenses, 3-D movie films, and other purposes.

Fannie Farmer: Cookbook

If Fannie Merritt Farmer (1857–1915) had not developed the case of polio at the age of 16 that left her left leg mildly paralyzed, American cuisine might have taken far longer to develop. The paralysis prevented her from either going to college or getting married. The result was that she turned to cooking at home. She developed such a talent for it that she eventually attended the Boston Cooking School, from which she graduated in 1889. She later served as the school's director from 1891 until 1902.

But Farmer's greatest accomplishment was the invention of the scientific, standardized recipe. For years, women had cooked using a pinch of this and a handful of that. Farmer realized that precise measurements would make recipes consistent and food more

▲ Fannie Farmer's system of level measurements and standard units for recipes simplified the whole business of cooking.

▼ A portrait of Fannie Merritt Farmer, one of America's best known cooking experts. Her cookbooks became classics and have sold millions of copies.

delicious. The book she edited, *The Boston Cooking School Cook Book* (1896), introduced teaspoons and tablespoons to the American public—and cooking was never the same again.

Farmer also edited a popular cooking column in the *Women's Home Companion* for ten years and gave her name to *The Fannie Farmer Cookbook*—one of the best-known cookbooks ever.

◀ *Fannie Farmer is seen here with one of her pupils, Martha Hayes Ludden, at the Boston Cooking School, where many recipes were formulated and kitchen tested.*

Whitcomb Judson, a Chicago engineer, thought he had found a winner when he invented the zipper and patented it in 1891. But he had to wait nearly 30 years before the design, often modified, caught on.

Judson's first zipper was called either a clasp locker or an unlocker. It had flat, hooklike, metal projections that interlocked, and was made to replace the many hooks and eyes of ladies' boots and shoes. Unfortunately, it was unreliable, often jamming or popping open. Two years later, Judson introduced interlocking teeth designed for clothes and fabrics, which he called C-curity! The zipper finally acquired its name from a shoe known as the zipper.

A Swedish engineer, Gideon Sundback, who was working for Judson in 1906, improved zippers by designing tiny cups, or hollows, at the backs of the interlocking teeth to hold them snugly together. A machine was later developed to stamp out metal teeth secured to fabric tape.

The Automatic Hook and Eye Company of Hoboken, New Jersey, improved the design some more. In 1918, a contract for the U.S. Navy for 10,000 zip fasteners for uniforms widened their popularity. Success was assured after B. F. Goodrich & Company put zippers into rain galoshes. Today, the main rival to the zipper is the Velcro touch-and-close fastener.

▼ *Close-up of the action of a modern zipper. The first zippers looked a bit like chain mail. They were made to fasten boots.*

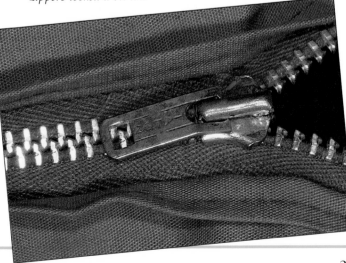

King Camp Gillette (1855–1932) never forgot the words an inventor named William Painter had once told him. He recalled them one morning when he was shaving: "If you invent something which people use and throw away, they will come back for more. And you will be a rich man."

Gillette, a traveling hardware salesman from Fond du Lac, Wisconsin, realized that only a small part of the "cut-throat" razor he was using was really necessary—the blade. Besides, every time he shaved, he ran the risk of gashing his face if someone knocked into his arm. Why not make a smaller, safer blade that could be thrown away afterward?

With the help of a mechanic friend, William Nickerson, Gillette designed a safety razor blade and holder and filed a patent for it in 1901. Since

◄ *No stropping, no honing— and this razor will give you "the most delightful shave" in three minutes, claims this advertisement.*

▲ *Shaving with a modern safety razor. Gillette intended only the blade of his original to be discarded; we now use disposable razors.*

only a narrow edge of the blade protruded from the holder, it could not inflict more than a minor nick in the event of an accident.

Safety razors were not originally a success. In 1904—Gillette and Nickerson's first year in business—they sold only 51 razors and 168 blades. However, their persistence was rewarded. Two years later, sales rocketed to 90,000 razors and 12,400,000 blades.

The electric razor was invented by Jacob Schick, a retired army officer, in 1928. His hand-held unit had a small electric motor that vibrated cutter blades backward and forward beneath a slatted foil through which the whiskers poked. Schick's electric razor was marketed in 1931 for $25, and different versions of the idea have been aggressively promoted by many other manufacturers ever since.

W. A. Cockran: Dishwasher

If an American woman had not been determined to market a machine that would free housewives (and their husbands) from the drudgery of washing the dishes, the dishwasher might not have been invented in 1889.

Mrs. W. A. Cockran, an Indiana housewife, had come up with the idea, essentially a wooden tub with a removable wire basket in which dishes could be stacked. Turning a handle would operate a pump on the outside of the machine, which would spray hot water over the dishes. Rollers inside the tub would turn the dishes.

Cockran's husband refused to put money into her "crazy idea." It was not until after his death ten years later that her dishwasher was produced. It quickly caught on. Larger machines driven by steam engines were eventually built, which were capable of "washing, scalding, rinsing, and drying up to two dozen dishes of all shapes and sizes in two minutes."

▲ Dishwashers have ended much kitchen sink drudgery for many people by doing the dishes at the touch of a switch.

▼ Where are they now? This sturdy, no-nonsense old dishwasher would have been used in a commercial setting.

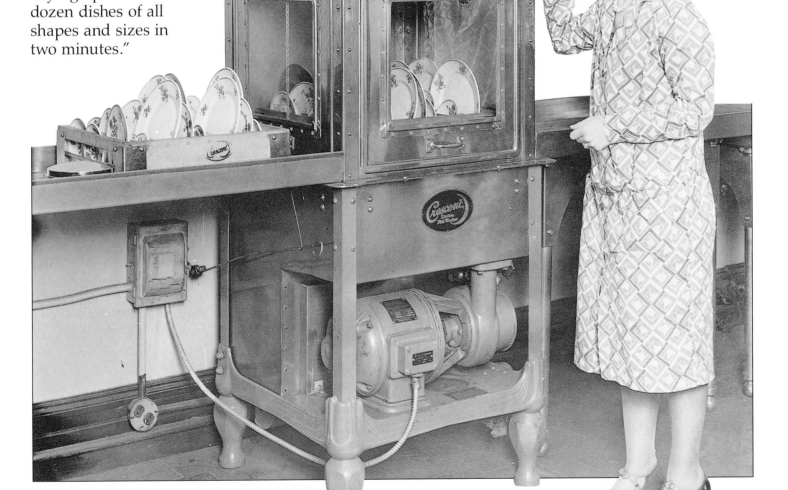

J. Murray Spangler: Vacuum cleaner

Vacuum cleaners of different types and sizes had been around on both sides of the Atlantic for a few years when a certain James Murray Spangler devised his own lightweight, motor-driven version in 1907. Spangler, from Canton, Ohio, was a janitor in a department store, and one of his duties was keeping the carpets clean. He found that the job aggravated his asthma. So he decided to install an electric fan inside his vacuum machine that would suck irritating dust into the machine and expel it into a collecting bag.

Unable to market the machine himself, he sold the rights in 1908 to a leather manufacturer named William Henry Hoover (1849–1932). Hoover soon began marketing the "upright" Hoover Model O cleaner, which ran on wheels and had a dust bag slung from its long handle. It was an immediate success. The company then introduced a roller that performed a beating action to loosen the dust as the machine passed over the carpets. This led to the famous slogan coined in 1919: "It beats as it sweeps as it cleans."

◀ *J. Murray Spangler was a store janitor when he invented the vacuum cleaner from a soap box, a goat-hair roller brush, a motorized fan, and a pillow case in which the dust was collected.*

◀ *A maid from a 1900s advertisement demonstrates an early vacuum cleaner in action. Some hand-driven machines used suction bellows.*

William Henry Hoover. ▲
His last name became
a household word.

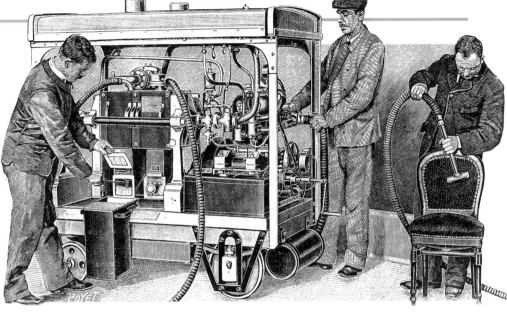

▲ One of the early large
commercial cleaners from
1903. Women hosted tea
parties while their homes
were cleaned.

▼ The rival Electric Sweeper-Vac,
as marketed by the Pneuvac
Company. The style of this
advertisement seems
quaint now.

Before you start Spring Cleaning

treat yourself to a New HOOVER CLEANER

Running a home these days is one of the hardest jobs going, and you're entitled to all the help you can get. So now, before Spring Cleaning, get rid of that old, out-of-date cleaner of yours and treat yourself to a *new* 'Hoover', and so get the benefit of all the latest features.

Remember, too, the 'Hoover' does so much *more* than ordinary vacuum cleaners. It cleans carpets *right down to the roots*, removing the trodden-in gritty dirt which cuts the pile. Thus, it makes carpets last longer. You will be delighted, too, with the extremely efficient cleaning tools for curtains, upholstery, etc. Ask your Hoover Dealer to demonstrate.

There is a Hoover Cleaner to suit every home. Prices, with cleaning tools, from 10 gns. to 22 gns. (plus tax). Hire Purchase available.

THE HOOVER DOES SO MUCH MORE THAN ORDINARY VACUUM CLEANERS

The Hoover Cleaner lifts every little section of the carpet from the floor in turn and, by means of the exclusive Hoover Agitator (above), gently beats it on a cushion of air. It thus extracts the harmful gritty dirt from the carpet roots.

The HOOVER CLEANER
REGD. TRADE MARK

It BEATS... *as it* Sweeps... *as it* Cleans

HOOVER LIMITED • PERIVALE • GREENFORD • MIDDLESEX

◀ Hoover's first Model O vacuum
cleaner. Hoover bought the
rights to the invention from
Spangler after the popularity of
automobiles diminished Hoover's
saddlery business.

▲ Even the British royal
family bought the
famous "It beats as it
sweeps as it cleans"
machine, as the coat of
arms shown here proves.

ONE perfected feature—the MOTOR DRIVEN BRUSH—is alone worth to you the entire price of the Electric SWEEPER-VAC. This efficient, soft brush (motor driven) revolves 1350 times per minute. It gets ALL lint, threads, hairs and embedded dirt, and, with Powerful Suction, draws them into the dust bag. Ask your dealer for the "Electric SWEEPER-VAC" (don't accept a substitute.) Give it a thorough test on your own rugs.

Pneuvac Company— 166 Fremont Street—Worcester, Mass.

WRITE for this free catalog, the most elaborate one ever written on Vacuum Cleaners.

Electric SWEEPER-VAC
With Motor Driven Brush

Robert Chesebrough: Vaseline

Visiting America's first oil-producing well in Titusville, Pennsylvania, in 1859, Robert Chesebrough (1837–1933), a research chemist, became curious about the colorless residue that formed around the rods of the pumps in use. He took home a sample with which to experiment in his laboratory. There, he was able to extract a wax, which he called petroleum jelly. Convinced that it had healing powers, he tested it out by inflicting scratches, cuts, and burns on his own body, then treating them with the soothing balm.

But he could not market his invention. People were afraid that containers of his petroleum jelly would explode! Eventually, he toured towns, handing out samples from an open carriage. Finally, the orders came pouring in. Petroleum jelly is still commonly used as a softening or soothing skin agent, in wound dressings, and as a barrier ointment to prevent sore skin. And Chesebrough, who swallowed a teaspoonful of his Vaseline every day, died in 1933 at the age of 96.

▼ *Chesebrough's worldwide advertising from the 1880s endeavored to popularize Vaseline. Some people at first feared petroleum jelly would explode!*

Raytheon: Microwave oven

◄ *The Radarange, one of Raytheon's early microwave ovens, as marketed to restaurants in 1948. It was a commercial application of the magnetron, which was developed during World War II.*

▼ *Dr. Percy Spencer, director of Raytheon's microwave and power-tube division, which developed the fast-cooking microwave oven in 1945*

The microwave oven is an example of an invention that started life designed to do one job and became most successful when used for another. In 1940, two scientists, Sir John Randall and Dr. H. A. M. Boot, were engaged in wartime research in the physics department of Birmingham University, England. There, they built what they called a magnetron. This device generated ultrashort electromagnetic waves, which are similar to those that transmit radio signals. The magnetron was devised to increase the range of radar for spotting enemy aircraft.

After the war, in 1945, the American Raytheon Manufacturing Company of Newton, Massachusetts, found that the electromagnetic waves from the magnetron changed the polarity of water molecules (including those in food). This made them vibrate very rapidly, which created the heat that cooked the food. The device Raytheon developed was patented in 1953 as a high-frequency dielectric heating apparatus. It is now universally known as the microwave.

Gregory Pincus: The Pill

Though couples have used a bewildering variety of contraceptive techniques since ancient days, they have long sought a simple pill that ensured safe and reliable contraception. In the 1950s, physiologist Dr. Gregory Pincus (1903–67) of Woodbine, New Jersey, developed the oral contraceptive. It is the most effective contraceptive the world has ever known.

Educated at Cornell and Harvard universities, Pincus was research director at the Worcester Foundation of Experimental Biology, in Shrewsbury, Massachusetts. To investigate female infertility, he studied the hormone-controlled, natural biological cycle of ovulation. In this cycle, an egg is released every month from one of a woman's two ovaries for fertilization by the male sperm. One hormone, the sex hormone called progesterone, is found in greater concentrations in pregnant women. Pincus and his colleagues discovered that if progesterone was given artificially to a woman, this would stop her from ovulating by tricking her body into believing she was already pregnant. Clinical trials resulted in the first Pill going on the market in 1957.

The make-up of today's oral contraceptives has changed considerably, although they are still based on sex hormones taken either singly or in combination. Single-hormone pills do not suppress ovulation but make the lining of the womb reject a fertilized egg. Almost 100 percent effective, oral contraceptives are extremely safe. But in certain people, they may cause side effects, such as thrombosis and high blood pressure (particularly in overweight smokers), and their long-term effects are still being studied.

A one-month pack of ▶ contraceptive pills. The rotating arrow points to successive days to ensure that no pill is missed.

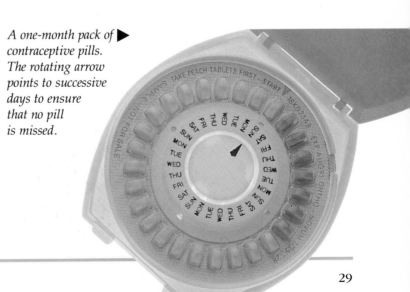

3 On the Move   *Robert Fulton: Steamboat*

It is not always enough to be the first person to invent something. Robert Fulton (1765–1815), for instance, was not the first to launch a steamboat. A French infantry officer and inventor, the Marquis Claude-François Dorotheé de Jouffroy d'Abbans (1791–1832), had already demonstrated a paddle steamboat in southeast France in 1783, but without an enthusiastic response. The American John Fitch (1743–98) also deserves some credit. He built a steamboat that traveled from Philadelphia to Trenton before it was destroyed in a storm in 1792. But it was Fulton who launched the first commercially successful steamboat . . . and is usually credited with its invention. As such, he has earned a place in the Hall of Fame of Great Americans.

Fulton was always inventing. As a boy of 14, he designed a manually operated paddleboat for fishing. And when he ordered a Boulton and Watt steam engine to be installed in a 133-foot paddleboat in 1806, he changed the course of maritime history. So successful was his design that the following year, his engine drove the ship *Clermont* 132 miles up the Hudson River from New York to Albany in just 32 hours. This was faster than any other river transport. Soon Fulton had a small fleet of passenger and cargo steamboats.

A man of prodigious talent, Fulton also invented a steam-powered warship, although it never saw action; a submarine torpedo boat (turned down by Napoléon I and the British); and a powered dredger for building canals. In addition, he was a successful painter of miniature portraits and landscapes.

◄ *Fulton's paddle steamer, the* Clermont, *traveled between New York and Albany on the Hudson River from 1807 onward.*

▲ *A portrait by Rembrandt Peale of Robert Fulton, engineer and inventor of the first successful paddle steamer in the world.*

James Finlay: Suspension bridge

Bridges have been used since the Stone Age. But the first suspension bridge made of chains or iron rods linked together by a horizontal deck or road was completed in 1801. It was built in the United States by James Finlay and spanned 70 feet over Jacob's Creek, Pennsylvania.

One of the world's most famous bridges is the Brooklyn Bridge, in New York, built by John Augustus Roebling (1806–69). It was opened in 1883. The first bridge to be suspended from steel cables, it has a span of 1,595 feet. Today, the world's longest suspension bridge is the Minami Bisan-seto Bridge in Japan. Opened in 1988, it has a span of 5,655 feet.

◀ The Clermont *being loaded and prepared for her first commercial voyage. Fulton also offered Napoléon I plans for a submarine.*

▼ *The Brooklyn suspension bridge against the Manhattan skyline. Suspension bridges weigh less and spread weight better than other types do.*

▼ *The Brooklyn Bridge, showing construction work in 1880. It was the first bridge to use steel wire— 1,200 miles of it.*

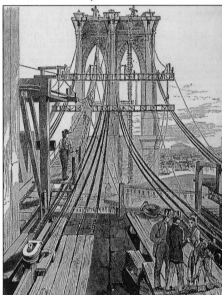

John Ericsson: Propeller

John Ericsson (1803–89) was a Swedish-American engineer and inventor whose ship's screw propeller, patented in 1836 while Ericsson was living in England, eventually replaced the paddle wheels that steamships relied on. Screw propellers were more efficient in rough water and, unlike paddle wheels, transmitted a constant load on ships' engines.

The propellers proved successful when fitted to a small U.S. Navy vessel built in Britain, which reached New York in 1839. In 1862, Ericsson launched an ironclad, self-propelled floating platform called the USS *Monitor*, which carried two 11-inch naval guns in a rotating turret. It battled the Confederate navy's ironclad CSS *Merrimac* in an epic duel in Hampton Roads, Virginia, in March of that year.

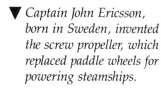

▼ *Nearly as big as a house, this giant propeller can drive a large oceangoing vessel. It transforms rotational force into thrust.*

The duel between Ericsson's ▶ *propeller-driven ship, the* Monitor, *and the Confederate navy's ironclad* Merrimac *in Hampton Roads, Virginia. Propellers were a major advance in ship design.*

▼ *Captain John Ericsson, born in Sweden, invented the screw propeller, which replaced paddle wheels for powering steamships.*

Elmer Ambrose Sperry (1860–1930) was a natural inventor, with 400 patents to his name. They ranged from military searchlights to electric locomotives and other devices. He was particularly interested in gyroscopes. Like a child's top, the gyroscope's wheel will always maintain the same orientation, even when the surface it rests on is tilted.

In 1910, Sperry designed a compass based on a gyroscopic wheel, which could point to true north and not be deflected by movement or the metal of a ship's hull. He fitted the first gyroscopic naval compass on the USS *Delaware* in 1911. It was so successful that orders poured in from navies around the world, with an enormous demand developing during World War I. After the war, merchant shipping clamored for his gyrocompasses.

In 1922, Sperry's invention led to "metal mike," a forerunner of a ship's automatic pilot based on the gyroscope principle. Later, Sperry developed a gyroscopic stabilizer for aircraft, which provided an artificial horizon. Today, aviators' automatic pilots, military aircraft control systems, and missile guidance systems are based on the principles of Sperry's invention.

▲ Ericsson in his study. He was a Swedish army engineer who moved to England in 1826 and subsequently emigrated to the United States in 1839.

Elmer Sperry, an electrical ▶ engineer who turned gyroscopes into navigational aids. He held 400 patents on various inventions.

Elisha Otis: Elevator

The famous skylines of New York and other skyscraper cities owe their existence to the humble elevator. The invention of the safety elevator by Elisha Graves Otis (1811–61) made it practical for the first time to construct buildings more than six stories high.

Otis was born in Halifax, Vermont, and became a mechanic at a New York bed factory. He was inspired to design a safety elevator when he was involved in moving equipment into his firm's new warehouse. Most elevators of the time were extremely dangerous. Otis's firm needed an elevator that could carry humans and equipment safely to the upper floors.

At the Crystal Palace Exposition in New York in 1853, Otis demonstrated just how safe the elevator he had built in 1852 was. While a large group of people watched from below, he rode up to a great height in his elevator. Once there, his assistant severed the cable supporting the elevator! But instead of crashing to the ground, the elevator stopped.

The key to his invention was that each side of his elevator shaft had a toothed guide rail running down it. The elevator cage was equipped with a single tooth, known as a pawl, on either side. Each pawl could engage with the guide rail, locking the elevator cage in place. If there was any failure of the tension of the cable holding the elevator, springs would automatically engage this pawl, preventing the cage from crashing downward. Today's elevators have claws that grab the track if the cable breaks, and the electric winding gear locks if the power supply is cut.

Otis subsequently established the Otis Steam Elevator Company. In 1857, he installed the world's first passenger elevator in the five-floor china shop of E. V. Haughwout & Company on Broadway.

Elisha Otis. His elevator ▶ *made skyscrapers possible. The world's first passenger elevator began operation in 1857.*

▲ *Traveling up the famous Eiffel Tower in Paris in (A) Otis's elevator car (with front cut away), which could carry 50 passengers. (B) Leg of the tower shows the angle of ascent.*

▼ *Elisha Otis demonstrates his elevator at the Crystal Palace, New York, 1853. With a flourish, he has just ordered the cable to be cut.*

Mary Anderson: Windshield wiper

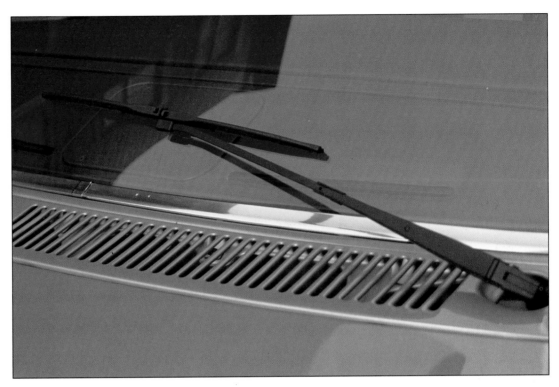

▼ *You need good visibility to drive big trucks like this. Mary Anderson's invention has made road travel much safer for us all.*

▲ *The windshield wiper on a modern automobile is precisely engineered. It has come a long way since 1902.*

New York was very proud of its electric trolleys at the turn of the century. They were the latest way to get around. But Mary Anderson, who visited New York from her native Birmingham, Alabama, in 1902, didn't like those trolleys at all. She thought they weren't safe.

It wasn't that the drivers were bad. It was the windshields. In those days, drivers rubbed their windshields with damp tobacco or an onion. This was supposed to help keep off rain and snow. But it didn't work too well. Anderson watched as the trolley drivers struggled to see out of their windshields, and came up with an idea.

Back in Alabama, Anderson created the first windshield wiper by attaching a handle to a rubber blade. This, in turn, was attached to the windshield. The driver had to turn the handle back and forth by hand to make the blade wipe off the rain. But the device worked. And travel in bad weather was made a little safer for everyone.

Henry Ford: Industrial production line

Industrialist Henry Ford (1863–1947) did not invent the automobile. But he was the originator of the world's first moving industrial production line. This enabled him to make reasonably priced cars, which made automobiles available to the masses. He ultimately became the largest automobile producer in the world. He made a fortune, and his name became a household word.

It all began when Ford was 13. The sight of a self-propelled steam engine in Dearborn, Michigan, fired his imagination, and he began to train as a mechanic. Afterward, he became a night engineer at the Detroit power plant of the Edison Illuminating Company to "learn about electricity" before building his first two-cylinder horseless carriage in 1893.

In 1903, he founded the Ford Motor Company to produce his automobiles. Among them was the famous Model T, designed in 1908. The car was sturdy and reliable, yet lightweight and easy to operate. It sold for $850 in 1908. Fifteen million would be sold by the time the model was discontinued, in 1928.

But early on, the factory couldn't turn out cars fast enough to meet demand. So Ford installed a slowly moving belt that allowed specialized workers to fit the same component quickly to each vehicle as it passed. This cut the time needed to fit a chassis together from fourteen hours to just over one and one-half, and for an alternator, from twenty minutes to five.

Soon Model Ts were being driven off the production line at the rate of one every 90 seconds. By 1915, Ford was turning out a million automobiles a year, and ten years later, he was able to bring down the price to $290. The era of the mass-produced automobile had begun.

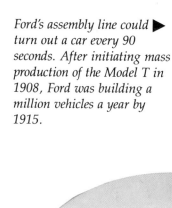

Ford's assembly line could ► *turn out a car every 90 seconds. After initiating mass production of the Model T in 1908, Ford was building a million vehicles a year by 1915.*

▲
Henry Ford, the man who pioneered cheap automobiles by inventing an assembly line that dramatically reduced the cost of a Model T

◄ *A modern auto assembly line with not a human welder in sight. Future factories may be staffed entirely by robots and a janitor.*

Wilbur and Orville Wright: Aviation

One of the most amazing things about the momentous moment in history when two Americans made human beings' first powered flight was that few people believed them! Reporters, who had not been present, thought they were being hoaxed. Two brothers who ran a bicycle shop in Dayton, Ohio—Wilbur Wright (1867–1912) and Orville (1871–1948)—couldn't have invented and flown the first successful airplane!

But they had. It happened on December 17, 1903. On that cold day above the breezy coastal sand dunes of Kill Devil Hills, Kitty Hawk, North Carolina, Orville eased their rickety biplane with its lightweight 12hp gasoline engine into the air for the first time. The flight lasted just 12 seconds. But by the end of the day, during which each brother made two flights in *Flyer 1*, the airplane was able to remain airborne for just under a minute and cover 850 feet.

It took a lot of ingenuity and a "feel" for aerodynamics for the brothers to get powered flight off the ground in barely seven years. They were enthusiastic cyclists—Orville was a competitive champion—who had taken up the daring sport of gliding. They were inspired to build their own aircraft following the death of Otto Lilienthal (1848–96), a German engineer who was killed in a glider accident.

▼ *The dramatic first flight at Kitty Hawk in 1903. Orville Wright is in the pilot's seat, while Wilbur runs alongside. The flight lasted 12 seconds.*

▲ *Wilbur Wright's first flight in Europe as represented in the French magazine* Le Petit Journal, *which was published in Paris on August 30, 1908.*

▲ Lieutenant Thomas Selfridge was the first man to die in a plane crash. On September 17, 1908, he was killed in this accident, while Wilbur Wright was injured.

A close-up of the Wright ▶ aircraft, with Wilbur (left), revealing its light frame. Note the rudimentary nature of the pilot's seat.

With natural mechanical aptitude but little technical training, the Wrights studied Lilienthal's and other researchers' exploits and writings. They designed an aircraft powered by an internal-combustion engine driving two rear-facing propellers. Then they built three gliders, employing a vertical rudder and a wing-warping system of their own design (wires that changed the shape of the wingtip during flight) to steer the plane. They exhaustively test-flew the gliders, checking design models in their own wind tunnel. Only then did they build and add the engine.

Despite their initial success, it was not until 1905 that the brothers could remain airborne for 30 minutes (and 24 miles). When Frenchman Louis Blériot (1872–1935) made the first 23½-mile solo crossing of the English Channel in his own monoplane four years later, the era of aviation was truly born. Aerial warfare during World War I, 1914–18, followed by Lindbergh's solo flight across the Atlantic in 1927, ensured that air travel had finally arrived.

▼ An Airbus A310 jet airliner, which is typical of modern aircraft today. It can trace its origins back to the Wright biplane of 1903.

Robert Goddard: Rocketry

Spaceships that can fly to the moon and shuttle astronauts into space owe their existence to a young man from Worcester, Massachusetts, who dreamed of building the world's most powerful rockets. Gunpowder rockets are said to have been used by Chinese soldiers in the 13th century. But Robert Hutchings Goddard (1882–1945), a physics professor at Clark University in Worcester, believed that liquid fuel could overcome the limitations of solid-fuel rockets of the day, providing reliable and controllable thrust.

A rocket must generate a powerful propulsive force known as thrust in order to gain height. This force can be generated by igniting a combination of a fuel and an oxidizer in the rocket engine. Goddard used liquid fuels such as gasoline and liquid oxygen as his oxidizer. On March 16, 1926, he launched the world's first successful liquid-fuel rocket. Not much bigger than a large firework, it reached an altitude of only 41 feet and landed 184 feet away from the launch site. But it demonstrated that his theories were correct. More flights followed at his "rocket range"—the farm of an aunt in Auburn, Massachusetts.

Goddard's scientific theories on sending rockets to the moon were ridiculed in the *New York Times*. He was also banned from further launches in the state because of the risks and noise they created. He therefore became more secretive about his work. In 1935, Goddard launched a liquid-fuel rocket that reached a height of 1.5 miles in the New Mexico desert. He thus founded a technology that has provided rockets to launch satellites, space probes, and defense payloads.

Goddard's 200 rocket patents included one for the first practical steering device for rockets, in which small rudders direct the gases of the jet exhaust. He also invented the antitank bazooka gun and jet-thrust boosters to assist fighters taking off from aircraft carriers.

Alice Chatham: Space helmet

The familiar and futuristic space helmets worn by all American astronauts owe their existence to Alice Chatham. A sculptor from Dayton, Ohio, Chatham was working for the U.S. Air Force during the time that Captain Chuck Yeager was trying to set new world records in his Bell X-1. She hand made the helmet worn by Yeager when he broke the sound barrier for the first time on October 14, 1947. She went on to design the astronauts' helmets.

▲ Captain Charles "Chuck" Yeager wearing the helmet designed by Alice Chatham. Yeager wore it when he broke the sound barrier in his X-1 airplane in 1947.

▼ Robert Goddard, the "father of rocketry," with his liquid oxygen/gasoline rocket, which made its first flight in Auburn, Massachusetts, on March 16, 1926

Wernher von Braun: Moon rocket

Wernher von Braun (1912–77), son of a rich German baron, began his working life as Hitler's chief rocket missile engineer during World War II. He ended his career as head of the team that launched America's first manned rocket to the moon.

At the Peenemünde experimental weapons center on the Baltic coast of Germany, von Braun developed guided weapons, including the V1 rocket "buzz bomb" and the V2 supersonic rocket, a 200-mile-range rocket that rose 60 miles high. Fueled by alcohol and lox (liquid oxygen), the first successful V2 flight broke all records for height, weight, speed, and range in 1942.

Von Braun surrendered to the Allied forces at the end of World War II. He then became an American citizen. He is best known for leading the NASA team dedicated to building the giant *Saturn V* moon rocket. It was this rocket that eventually carried Neil Armstrong and Buzz Aldrin to the moon in July 1969.

◀ *Germany's Dr. Wernher von Braun, the brilliant rocket engineer who headed the NASA rocket team that built the Saturn V moon rocket*

▲ *This is where Goddard's work has led. A Delta II liquid-fuel rocket launches the Roentgen Satellite (ROSAT) in June 1990.*

4 Weapons and Warfare   *David Bushnell: Submarine*

The first reliable submarine appears to have been built in the 1620s, when Dutchman Cornelius Drebbel demonstrated his leaky vessel with a hull of greased leather. It was powered by 12 rowers.

But it is David Bushnell (c. 1742–1824), an 18th-century engineer and inventor from Saybrook, Connecticut, who is considered to be the "father of the modern submarine." He was not the first man to build one, but his design in 1776 proved to be the most successful. And his wooden submarine, *Turtle*, powered by two hand-turned screws, made the first submarine attack in history.

Bushnell's advanced, turtle-shaped vessel had buoyancy tanks that flooded for submerging and were pumped out to surface, as do submarines today. It could be armed with a mine or a torpedo that would attach to the hull of an enemy ship. The *Turtle* introduced the world to underwater warfare during the American Revolution, when it made an attack on the British warship *Eagle* in New York's harbor. It attempted to attach a mine to the ship, but the boring device controlled from inside the *Turtle* could not penetrate the *Eagle's* copper hull.

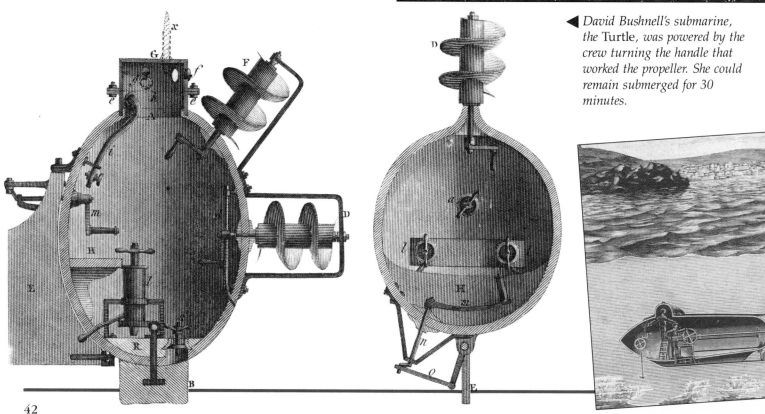

◀ *David Bushnell's submarine, the* Turtle, *was powered by the crew turning the handle that worked the propeller. She could remain submerged for 30 minutes.*

Bushnell's principles were later used by Robert Fulton when he built a military submarine. Fulton's cigar-shaped vessel, made in 1800 from copper sheets stretched over iron ribs, was powered by a crew of three who hand-cranked propellers. Like a modern submarine, it had horizontal rudders—now called hydroplanes—to steer the vessel up and down. Called the *Nautilus*, it successfully operated in France during 1800 and 1801. It dove to 25 feet and had a four-hour air supply and a range of several miles.

Today's American nuclear-powered submarines, descendants of Bushnell's frail craft, have traveled under the North Pole ice cap and can remain submerged for months at a time.

◄ *The USS* Grayback *was converted into a transport submarine. U.S. special forces could be launched from her in midget submarines.*

▼ *A deadly descendant of Bushnell's submarine, this is USS* Miami, *one of the latest of the nuclear-powered Los Angeles-class submarines.*

▼ *The submarine* Nautilus, *designed by Robert Fulton, seen submerged (1), and traveling on the surface (2). She was powered by hand-cranked propellers.*

Samuel Colt: Revolver

A piece of whittling wood and a knife are said to have made Samuel Colt (1814–62), inventor of the revolver, one of America's richest men. Born the son of a silk merchant in Hartford, Connecticut, young Colt had an innovative mind. On one occasion, he blew a raft out of a local pond with underwater explosives. He was also expelled for damaging his school in another explosive experiment.

He ran away to sea at 16 and sailed to Calcutta, India, where he came across a primitive revolving pistol made by one Elisha Collier. Back on ship, it is said that Colt got the idea for perfecting the mechanism of a revolving gun breech by watching the ratchet-and-pawl mechanism of the winch as it wound up the anchor. He immediately fashioned a working revolver from a piece of wood. With his father's backing, Colt later made a prototype gun with a cylindrical cartridge magazine that revolved between the hammer and the barrel. With each pull of the trigger, the cylinder revolved, automatically positioning a new round so it was ready to fire.

Patented in 1835, the rapid-fire Colt six-shot .36-caliber revolver led to widescale use of hand weapons in America. Colt set up the Patent Arms Manufacturing Co., but it went bankrupt in its early years. He got another chance following the outbreak of the Mexican War in 1846. In 1847, the U.S. Mounted Rifles ordered 1,000 .44-caliber Colts. Then they ordered another 1,000. Colt set up a second factory and made a fortune manufacturing guns and rifles.

Colt also devised the first remote-control underwater mine in 1843 and helped advance marine telegraph communications.

Samuel Colt, ▶ *inventor of the revolver, dabbled with explosives before making his fortune inventing firearms for military and civil use.*

The inventor holds his famous ▶ *revolver. The rapid-fire six-shot .36-caliber revolver became popular all across America, although initially sales were slow.*

▲ Colt's original revolver, cocked and ready to shoot. Each time the hammer was pulled back, the cylinder turned and positioned another bullet.

▼ Buffalo Bill Cody shoots a Native American with a revolver. This picture was published in the Petit Journal Supplément Illustré, Paris, 1890, at which time Cody was touring Europe in a Wild West show.

Richard Gatling: Machine gun

Since Richard Jordan Gatling (1818–1903) was trained as a doctor, it is curious that he should have invented the first successful machine gun, capable of killing on a mass scale. It is also surprising that when Dr. Gatling first offered his design of a rapid-fire, self-loading weapon to the Union army, the Ordnance Department showed little enthusiasm. The North was obviously suspicious of Gatling, who was born in the Confederate state of North Carolina. But eventually the army was convinced of the merits of the gun and used it experimentally in the Civil War.

The first version of Gatling's gun, patented in 1861, looked like a large rifle that could be mounted either on a tripod or on two large wheels like a cannon. But instead of a single rifle barrel, the gun had six to ten barrels grouped in circular formation. As the operator turned a handle, the barrels revolved past the firing mechanism and released up to 1,000 rounds a minute. Ammunition was supplied automatically from a carousel-like magazine holding 240 rounds above the turning barrels. Each round dropped into a barrel for firing in turn, and empty cartridges were automatically ejected.

Gatling also invented an agricultural sowing machine and a steam plow, but his name has entered the language because of his military invention.

▲ *Gatling guns became popular abroad. Here, a gun is fitted to the saddle of a camel, one of the more improbable machine gun mounts in military history!*

Richard Jordan Gatling was ▶ *trained as a doctor but was more interested in mechanical engineering.*

◀ *Gatling's wheel-mounted machine gun pictured in 1872. It was the first successful machine gun and was used during the Civil War. The czar of Russia ordered 400 of these guns.*

John Moses Browning ▶ *(left), inventor of the automatic rifle used in both world wars. The gun, with a 20-round magazine, gave troops the fast reloading rifle they needed.*

John Browning: Automatic rifle

John Moses Browning (1855–1926) was one of the world's leading gun designers. Born in Ogden, Utah, he was inventive even as a child. He made his first gun at the age of 13 in his father's gun shop. In 1879, when he was in his mid-20s, he patented a single-shot rifle, which he and his brother sold to the Winchester Repeating Arms Company. Other commercially successful weapon designs followed for major arms companies.

World War I demonstrated the need for an automatic rifle that soldiers did not need to reload manually as they advanced on the enemy. Browning produced such a weapon, which was adopted by the U.S. Army in 1918 and saw service until the late 1950s. This was a .30-caliber automatic rifle with a magazine holding 20 cartridges. It could fire single shots or automatically. The recoil of the gun on firing a round caused a piston rod to release the bolt mechanism, pushing it back to extract the empty case. Then the bolt was pushed forward by a spring to load a fresh round.

Browning was a master of design. He produced all kinds of weapons, from pistols, machine guns, and shotguns and ammunition to antiaircraft artillery. Weapons that he designed were manufactured by Remington, Colt, Winchester, and European gunmakers. Browning died in Herstal, Belgium, in 1926.

J. Robert Oppenheimer: Nuclear bomb

The nuclear bomb is one of the most momentous inventions of mankind. Nuclear power has given us a vast potential to harness a source of abundant energy. Misused, it can bring about world destruction. The nuclear, or atomic, bomb was developed at the Los Alamos research laboratory under the direction of Professor J. Robert Oppenheimer (1904–67) as part of a program code-named the Manhattan Project. It was first tested over the New Mexico desert on July 16, 1945. The following month, two atomic bombs ended World War II when they were dropped on Hiroshima and Nagasaki, Japan.

Oppenheimer was the Harvard-educated son of German immigrants. After spending some years researching in European countries, he returned to the United States in 1929. There, he divided his time between teaching at the California Institute of Technology and the University of California at Berkeley. In 1942, he set up and took charge of the Los Alamos laboratory. He remained there until 1945. In 1947, he was appointed director of the Institute for Advanced Study in Princeton, New Jersey.

In the first years of the war, Allied scientists explored the idea of making a powerful bomb by splitting atoms—the smallest particles of an element that can take part in a chemical reaction. America and Britain combined their research programs under the direction of Professor Oppenheimer. In 1945, they developed the world's most powerful bomb, made with uranium 235 and equivalent to 20,000 tons of the explosive TNT.

An atomic explosion is caused by a chain reaction of splitting atoms, which then split other atoms almost instantaneously. In the bomb, uranium 235 is packed into two separate compartments positioned at opposite ends of a container something like a gun barrel. On detonation, the two lumps of uranium 235 are fired into each other, starting a chain reaction. One atom of uranium 235 splits into two fragments under the impact of an individual neutron particle, causing it to release more neutrons. These released neutrons immediately split more atoms, which in turn release more neutrons in a self-sustaining sequence that takes only a tiny fraction of a second. This causes a sudden and massive release of energy.

From 1946 to 1952, Oppenheimer served as chairman of the advisory committee to the U.S. Atomic Energy Commission. Despite the success of the bombs in ending the war against Japan, Oppenheimer strongly objected to the creation of the even more devastating hydrogen bomb. He was declared a security risk and dismissed in 1953. He continued on as director of Princeton's Institute for Advanced Study.

▼ *Fireball of the hydrogen bomb test at Bikini Atoll on May 21, 1956—photographed from an aircraft 50 miles from the target*

J. Robert Oppenheimer ▶ *photographed in 1954, nine years after his atomic bombs had laid to waste much of Hiroshima and Nagasaki in Japan*

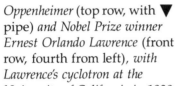

Oppenheimer (top row, with ▼ pipe) and Nobel Prize winner Ernest Orlando Lawrence (front row, fourth from left), with Lawrence's cyclotron at the University of California in 1939

▲ *Surface effects of the underwater explosion of the nuclear warhead of an Asroc missile fired from the USS Agerholm on exercise*

Returning from Europe in 1832, Samuel Finley Breese Morse (1791–1872), a successful portrait painter, saw a fellow passenger on the ship demonstrating an electrical apparatus bought in Europe. A year earlier, the English scientist Michael Faraday (1791–1867) had discovered how magnets could be used to create electricity.

Immediately, Samuel Morse had the idea to develop an electric telegraph system that could send messages by a coded arrangement of dots and dashes. Before the ship docked, he had filled notebooks with his ideas. Three years later, he built a working model of his electric telegraph device. Although not entirely original—a number of inventors, including William Cooke and Sir Charles Wheatstone of England, were building their own versions—his was the first complete design. In 1938, he created Morse code, which assigned different combinations of dots and dashes to each letter of the alphabet.

Morse became rich and famous for inventing this system, which saved countless lives at sea. It communicated by radio international events the same day, kept shipping in contact with the shore, and brought many fleeing murderers to justice.

▲ *Samuel Morse, inventor and portrait painter. His idea of the electric telegraph was quickly followed by the invention of Morse code.*

▼ *An extract from Morse's 1840-patented system of Morse code. Messages were transmitted in a series of dots and dashes by telegraph.*

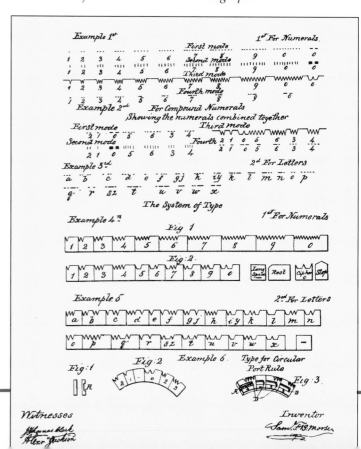

Lee De Forest: Radio vacuum tube

◄ *Lee De Forest displays his audio and oscillating tube. His invention enabled radio waves to be transmitted long distances for the first time.*

Lee De Forest, inventor ► *of the radio vacuum tube. It boosted voice transmissions over vast distances.*

In the early days of radio, scientists were unable to transmit strong radio signals over long distances. The signals became weak and distorted. Then Lee De Forest (1873–1961), a physicist and inventor from Council Bluffs, Iowa, invented a vacuum tube in 1906 that amplified radio signals so that they could be broadcast long distances for the first time. De Forest is often thought of as the "father of radio."

Called the three-electrode (or triode) vacuum tube, De Forest's invention drew upon the electrode technology of Edison's light bulb. The triode allowed transmitters and receivers to be much more sensitive. Vacuum tubes are still used today for television and other radio transmission, although much of their function was displaced by the invention of the transistor in 1947.

Reginald Fessenden: Radiotelephone

One day near Christmastime in 1906, ships' radio operators off the Massachusetts coast were startled to hear the sound of music and speech coming from their radiotelegraphy receivers. Only afterward did they discover that they were listening to history in the making. It was the first demonstration by Canadian-born Reginald Aubrey Fessenden (1866–1932) of radiotelephony. His advance, which led to the establishment of transatlantic telephone service, was made possible by a vacuum tube carrying the human voice on radio waves (*see also* Lee De Forest, page 51).

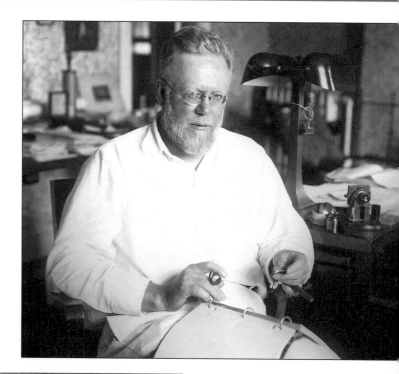

▼ *Alexander Graham Bell, the inventor, using a telephone system that still bears his name. This one was called the Centennial model.*

Reginald Fessenden, the ▶ Canadian-American physicist who made radiotelephones feasible. In 1906, he used radio waves to transmit voices.

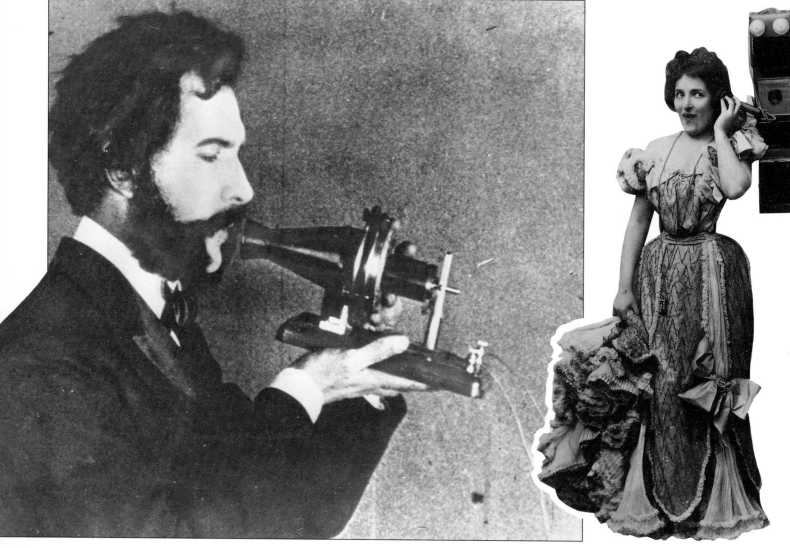

Alexander Graham Bell: Telephone

Today, you can pick up the telephone and talk to almost anyone in the world. With a radiotelephone hookup, a businessperson can be called in a car or aboard a ship or aircraft. The president can even chat with astronauts on the moon. In the future, you will not just call friends' homes or offices. You will call them *personally*. Their telephones will be worn on their wrists!

The originator of all this technology was an immigrant from Scotland, Alexander Graham Bell (1847–1922). In his early days, Bell was a teacher of the deaf. He soon became interested in acoustics and, later, voice transmission. Bell's approach to sending the human voice down a wire was to speak into a device that vibrated a strip of metal in response to different notes of speech, much like a reed in a musical instrument. When the reed was positioned close to an electromagnet, the voice vibrations were transmitted in the form of a varying electric current along the wire. This current activated in a similar way a receiving metal strip with an electromagnet. It thus reproduced the voice.

An accident in 1876 informed Bell that he had produced the first telephone based on this discovery. After spilling battery acid on his leg, he spoke into the machine, "Watson, come here, I want you!"—and his assistant came hurrying in from another laboratory. Bell patented his machine just hours before a rival inventor did his. Later, Thomas Edison produced a telephone with a separate mouthpiece and a more powerful transmitter, which could be used over longer distances. Bell himself also invented the microphone and loudspeaker.

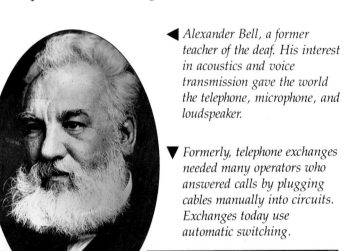

◄ *Alexander Bell, a former teacher of the deaf. His interest in acoustics and voice transmission gave the world the telephone, microphone, and loudspeaker.*

▼ *Formerly, telephone exchanges needed many operators who answered calls by plugging cables manually into circuits. Exchanges today use automatic switching.*

◄ *Soon after telephones were introduced, they became more than just a means of communication. They launched a new habit of social chatting.*

▼ *Pay phones enable calls to be made almost anywhere. In the future, say scientists, your phone will be worn on your wrist.*

Vladimir Zworykin: Television camera

Credit for the invention of television is usually given to the Scotsman John Logie Baird (1888–1946), who demonstrated his moving picture machine in 1926. But there was at least one man who came before. Vladimir Zworykin (1889–1982) fled the Russian Revolution in 1917. He joined the Westinghouse Electric Company in 1919 and became an American citizen in 1924. Fascinated by the idea of television, he developed the first electronic-scanning TV camera. He called it the iconoscope.

Zworykin's basic TV system, using the cathode-ray technology of the German Karl Ferdinand Braun (1850–1918), was able to transmit a picture to a kinescope screen—the picture tube of today. This was three years before Baird's demonstration.

Today's modern television camera focuses light from the subject onto a signal plate. This plate is made up of thousands of tiny squares of special material that respond to light by creating an electrical charge. The stronger the light, the bigger the charge. By scanning the signal plate rapidly line by line with a beam of electrons (small electrically charged particles), the picture image can be turned into electrical signals. These are transmitted as radio waves from the TV station.

Inside your home TV receiver, the process is reversed. The signals are converted back to electron beams, and a special coating inside the TV tube glows briefly according to the strength of the electron beams rapidly scanning it. This forms the moving picture. With color television, three sets of signals are transmitted, one each for the colors blue, red, and green.

An early television set with a circular screen. Today, the cathode-ray tube has a rectangular shape to fit the picture. Credit for pioneering today's television system goes to Scotsman John Logie Baird, who demonstrated moving television pictures in 1926.

Vladimir Zworykin with his invention, a forerunner of today's cathode-ray tube. In 1923, he produced an electronic camera called the iconoscope, which transmitted a picture.

Penicillin attacking bacteria ▶
was revealed by this large
electron microscope using an
electron camera. It is
demonstrated by Dr. Zworykin
of RCA (right) and Dr. James
Hilliard.

▼ *A modern television brings*
sports into the home from
anywhere in the world.
Camera crews can transmit
international events live via
satellites.

6 Electronics and Science

Without lightning conductors, no home, office, or factory would be safe from lightning strikes. The American statesman Benjamin Franklin (1706–90) is the inventor we can thank. He developed lightning rods following his now-famous 1752 experiment, in which he flew a kite made from a large silk handkerchief in a thunderstorm. By attaching a key to the kite, which emitted sparks when he placed his hand near it, Franklin was able to show that lightning was in fact a natural electrical discharge. The current traveled down the wet cord through his body to the earth.

It is important to note that Franklin did not know how dangerous this experiment was. It easily could have killed him and others nearby. (Others who tried the experiment were indeed killed.) So do not be tempted to repeat his experiment—or even to fly a kite during a thunderstorm!

▼ *A portrait of Benjamin Franklin in his study by painter Charles Willson Peale. Franklin invented the lightning conductor and bifocal glasses.*

Benjamin Franklin's famous experiment in 1752 used a key and a kite flown in a thunderstorm. It showed that lightning is a form of electricity. ▶

Benjamin Franklin: Lightning conductor

The first lightning rod that Franklin built consisted of a metal electrical conducting wire attached to the topmost part of a building near where he lived in Philadelphia. The wire ran to the ground, allowing the electricity to be conducted harmlessly to the earth.

Franklin also formulated the idea of positive and negative electrical current. Then, while ambassador to France in 1785, he invented bifocal glasses. Older people often develop both nearsightedness and farsightedness, requiring two pairs of glasses. By having one lens at the top of each eyepiece and another at the bottom, Franklin was able to see clearly both looking down (to read) and looking up—wearing just one pair of spectacles.

Franklin—a publisher, inventor, and statesman—served America in more ways than practically anyone else in American history.

▼ Benjamin West's artistic cherubs surrounding Franklin and his lightning conductor might have been prophetic. The experiment could have killed him!

In 1834, an English mathematician, Charles Babbage (1792–1871), prepared plans for a mechanical device that he called an analytical engine. It was designed to have a memory and to carry out many of the calculations of a modern computer. It would have been programmed with punched cards and would have printed out the results. But Babbage's ideas were before his time. He failed in his attempts to construct a machine because of the complexity of its working parts.

Computers as we know them began life as automatic electronic digital calculators. They were originally introduced to speed up commercial activities such as accounting. Hand-operated adding machines had been around since 1642, with keyboards added in America in 1850. But the forerunners of the modern computer did not appear until nearly the middle of this century. In 1942, John Atanasoff and Clifford Berry, at Iowa State University, invented an electronic digital calculator employing vacuum tubes, which was capable of speedy calculations and processing data. Two years later, Howard Hathaway Aiken (1900–1973), a mathematician and inventor, produced the Harvard Mark I computer. It was 51 feet long, 8 feet high, and weighed 35 tons, with 500 miles of wire circuits and 3 million connections. The computer was programmed by paper tape on which were coded instructions, though some manual switching was needed.

Charles Babbage: ahead of ▶ his time. His analytical engine was so complex, it was never finished.

In 1946, John von Neumann (1903–57) introduced the concept of a stored computer program at the Institute for Advanced Study in Princeton, New Jersey. Instead of using punched tape, the instructions and data were all kept in a common memory.

Around the same time, John Presper Eckert, an electrical engineer, together with John William Mauchly (1907–1980), built what is regarded as the first true electronic computer, at the University of Pennsylvania. It was capable of 5,000 simple calculations per second. Called the Electronic Numerical Integrator and Computer (ENIAC), it was a massive device with 18,000 vacuum tubes, requiring considerable electrical power. Because of overheating and other problems, the machine, which was intended to be used for military gunnery calculations, was unreliable.

Today, computers can have speeds of 10,000 megaflops, or 10,000 million operations a second. That is 2 million times faster than ENIAC.

◄ Howard Aiken, Nobel Prize winner, who constructed the Harvard Mark I calculating machine, a forerunner of the modern computer. It was used by the U.S. Navy for gunnery ballistics and design.

John Eckert, co-designer of ► the electronic computer, and James Weiner, his chief engineer, checking over their binary automatic computer in 1949

▼ Banks of machines in the computer room of the Chrysler Corporation.

Computers today can order stock and run a factory line.

◄ Part of Babbage's machine, a mechanical ancestor of the modern computer, which used cogs and gears. It was far in advance of adding machines.

▲ Dr. John Mauchly, co-inventor of the ENIAC computer, sets the machine to solve a mathematical problem at 5,000 operations per second.

Theodore Maiman: Laser

The laser—short for *light amplification by stimulated emission of radiation*—is a powerful light beam, or pulse, with a wide range of uses. Depending on the type of laser, it can slice through metals, weld or bore holes for industry, guide bombs to targets with pinpoint accuracy, and be used as a surgical scalpel. Lasers can also be used to make precision measurements over vast distances and to send millions of telephone and television signals between any two points in visual contact.

Lasers produce light that, unlike ordinary light, is "coherent." This means that all the photons (or particles of light) have the same wavelength, and all the light waves are in phase with one another. Because of this, they reinforce one another and can develop great energy. Theodore Maiman, a physicist born in Los Angeles, developed his pulsed ruby laser in 1960. Maiman produced his laser beam by exciting the atoms within a ruby to produce brief pulses of pure red light 10 million times more powerful than sunlight. He did this by stimulating the atoms with radiation from a high-energy light source.

In the same year came the gas laser, which produces a continuous light beam rather than a pulsed beam. It was developed by D. R. Herriott, A. Javan, and W. R. Bennett at Bell Telephone Laboratories.

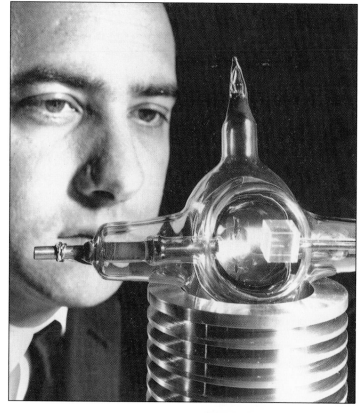

▲ Dr. Theodore Maiman of Hughes Research Laboratories with his laser invention, which produced a light source "brighter than the sun"

▼ A laser in action. Lasers are routinely used for cutting, measuring distances, reading bar codes, performing surgery, and even guiding weapons.

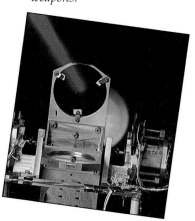

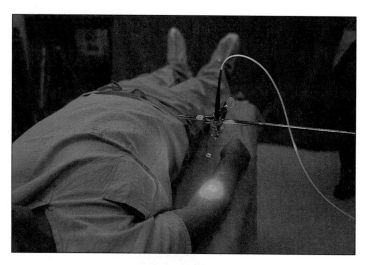

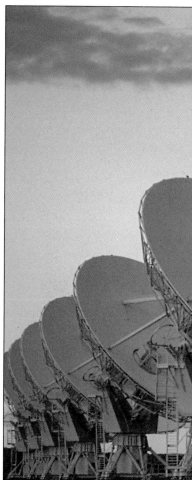

◄ Lasers are now used in hospitals for cleaning out blocked heart vessels, vaporizing diseased skin tissue, and removing tattoos.

Grote Reber: Radio telescope

If it had not been for a young American engineer's research program in 1931, which was aimed at finding out the cause of crackle and other interference with radio signals during thunderstorms, astronomers would not have found out so much about events in the deepest corners of our universe. In 1931, Karl Guthe Jansky (1905–50), an employee of Bell Telephone Laboratories, built a large aerial that swiveled on wheels taken from a Model T Ford. To his surprise, he discovered that part of the radio "noise" he picked up was not coming from thunderstorms, but from far away in the Milky Way galaxy. Jansky did not follow up this discovery.

In 1937, Grote Reber, a radio engineer from Illinois, built a 31-foot dish aerial to collect these radio signals. His device then converted them into electrical energy, whose strength could be plotted on a graph. It turned out that the radio signals came from many parts of the universe.

While optical telescopes gathered only visible light, radio telescopes could probe even deeper into space. Astronomers attempted to improve upon them by combining series of radio telescope aerials in groups, or arrays, so that together they acted like one massive telescope. In Socorro, New Mexico, a huge system of 27 radio telescopes called the Very Large Array (VLA) has been built in the shape of the letter Y with arms 12 to 13 miles long.

Scientists also make their radio telescopes more powerful by building larger and larger dishes. Today, the world's largest single-dish radio telescope at Arecibo, Puerto Rico, has a dish 1,000 feet in diameter. Radio telescopes have been used to make a number of remarkable discoveries, including the existence of pulsars in 1956. Even bigger radio telescopes may someday be erected in space, revealing further mysteries of the cosmos.

◀ Some of the 27 dish antennae that make up the VLA—the world's largest radio telescope in New Mexico

▼ The Parkes radio telescope in New South Wales, Australia, is rotated during maintenance work. Its dish is 210 feet in diameter.

Without computers, modern cities and industrial centers would shudder to a halt. Without silicon chips, there would be no modern computers. Silicon chips, sometimes known as integrated circuits, consist of many transistors integrated together in a single unit. The transistors upon which all this technology is based were invented by three scientists working together in America: Walter Brattain (1902–87), John Bardeen (1908–91), and William Shockley (1910–89), a British-born physicist.

In 1947, while working at Bell Telephone Laboratories, they built the first transistor, which acted like a vacuum tube, amplifying a radio signal. But it was much smaller than a vacuum tube and used far less current. For their invention, the three men shared the Nobel Prize for physics in 1956.

Transistors are electronic components made up of materials called semiconductors, which can act as switches to control the flow and direction of electricity passing through them. Semiconductors commonly consist of tiny sandwiches of germanium or silicon, so that alternate layers have different electrical properties.

In the early 1950s, transistors—much more reliable and requiring less power and less space—started to replace vacuum tubes in radios, computers, and other electronic equipment. Eventually, whole circuits, together with transistors, were placed on one tiny silicon chip. Modern silicon chips consist of millions of transistors, all contained in a package smaller than a fingernail.

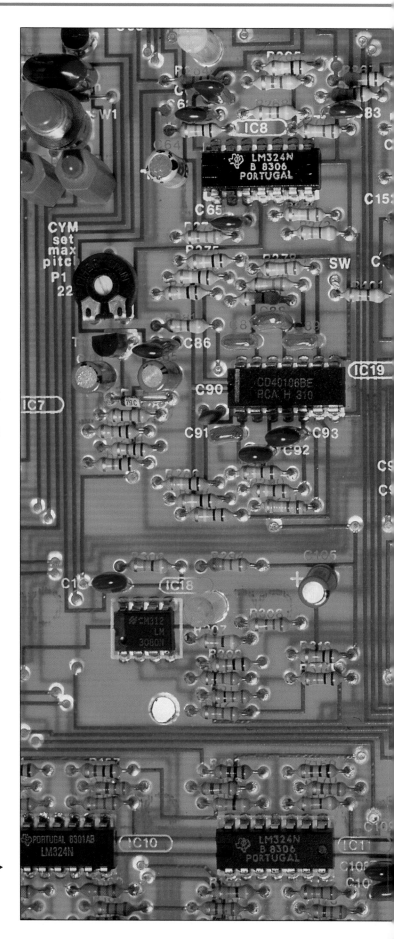

◀ *A colorful assortment of transistors. These components are the building blocks of radios, televisions, and other electronic equipment.*

A close-up of components on a ▶ *computer's circuit board. Small and efficient, such devices have revolutionized electronics.*

Jack Kilby: Integrated circuit

In 1958, ten years after the transistor was invented, Jack Kilby of Texas Instruments produced a circuit built from a single silicon crystal. He used silicon because it could be modified by adding different chemicals to it, which made pathways along which electricity could flow in a controllable manner. This created a miniaturized circuit of many interconnected electronic components, now known as a silicon chip, or an integrated circuit.

A handful of ▶ transistors, capacitors, and resistors—miniaturized components of modern electronic equipment

▼ *Part of a typical chip used in telecommunications* systems. *Each one contains entire electronic circuits.*

Further Reading about Inventors and Inventions

Aaseng, Nathan. *The Inventors: Nobel Prizes in Chemistry, Physics, and Medicine.* Minneapolis: Lerner Publications Company, 1988.

Garrison, Webb. *Why Didn't I Think of That? From Alarm Clocks to Zippers.* Englewood Cliffs, N.J.: Prentice-Hall, Inc., 1977.

Kerrod, Robin. *Science & Technology.* New York: Smithmark Publishers Inc., 1991.

Lafferty, Peter. *The Big Book of How Things Work.* New York: Gallery Books, 1990.

Macauley, David. *The Way Things Work.* Boston: Houghton Mifflin Company, 1988.

Murphy, Jim. *Guess Again: More Weird & Wacky Inventions.* New York: Bradbury Press, 1986.

Taylor, Ron. *Journey Through Inventions.* New York: Smithmark Publishers Inc., 1991.

Picture Credits

Index